My World of Science

HUMAN GROWTH

Angela Royston

Heinemann
LIBRARY

www.heinemann.co.uk/library
Visit our website to find out more information about **Heinemann Library** books.

To order:
☏ Phone 44 (0) 1865 888066
🖹 Send a fax to 44 (0) 1865 314091
🖵 Visit the Heinemann Bookshop at www.heinemann.co.uk/library to browse our catalogue and order online.

First published in Great Britain by Heinemann Library, Halley Court, Jordan Hill, Oxford OX2 8EJ, part of Harcourt Education.

Heinemann is a registered trademark of Harcourt Education Ltd.

Editorial: Andrew Farrow and Dan Nunn
Design: Jo Hinton-Malivoire and
    Tinstar Design Limited (www.tinstar.co.uk)
Picture Research: Maria Joannou and Sally Smith
Production: Viv Hichens

Originated by Blenheim Colour Ltd
Printed and bound in China by
    South China Printing Company

ISBN 0 431 13727 7
07 06 05 04 03
10 9 8 7 6 5 4 3 2 1

British Library Cataloguing in Publication Data
Royston, Angela
Human growth. – (My world of science)
1. Human growth – Juvenile literature
I. Title
621.6

A full catalogue record for this book is available from the British Library.

Acknowledgements
The publishers would like to thank the following for permission to reproduce photographs: Greg Evans International p. **11**; Network/Jenny Matthews p. **21**; Photodisc p. **7**; Pictor International p. **23**; Powerstock pp. **10, 20**; Robert Harding Picture Library p. **19**; Science Photo Library pp. **9** (BSIP, Laurent), **16, 18** (BSIP Chassenet), **28** (BSIP, LECA); Trevor Clifford pp. **4, 5, 6, 8, 12, 13, 15, 17, 22, 24, 25, 26, 27, 29**; Unknown p. **14**.

Cover photograph reproduced with permission of Ace Photo Agency.

Every effort has been made to contact copyright holders of any material reproduced in this book. Any omissions will be rectified in subsequent printings if notice is given to the publishers.

Contents

Any words appearing in the text in bold, **like this**,
are explained in the Glossary.

Growing bigger

When you were born you were a tiny baby. You grew bigger and heavier until you reached the size you are now.

You will continue to grow all the time you are a child. Sometimes you will grow faster than others. When you stop growing, you will be a 'grown up'!

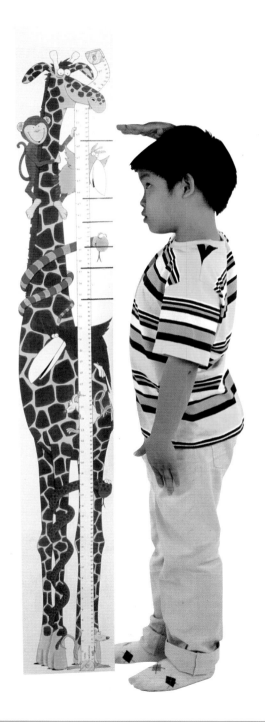

Changing size

Babies are different sizes when they are born. Most are around 50 centimetres long. That is even smaller than this teddy bear.

Babies and **toddlers** grow fast. When they are three years old, they are more than half the **height** of their **parents**!

Changing weight

As well as growing taller, you become heavier. You probably weighed about 3.5 kilograms when you were born. That is less than this bottle of water.

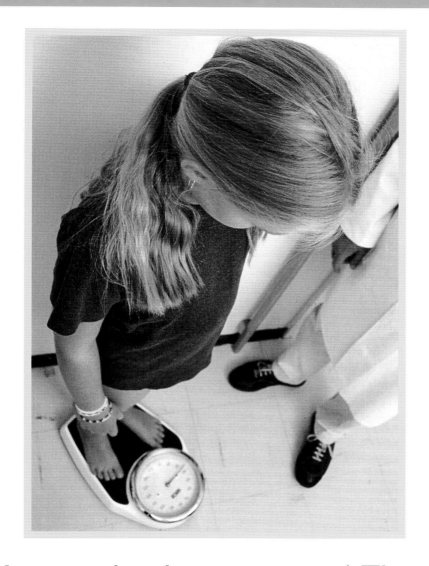

You weigh a lot more now! This girl is being weighed by the school nurse. The nurse checks that she weighs about the right amount for her age.

Changing shape

Your body changes shape as you grow. A baby's head is big compared to the rest of its body. Its arms and legs are short.

A **toddler's** arms and legs grow faster than the rest of its body. When you are about six years old, your legs are nearly half your **height**.

How tall will you grow?

Children grow at different rates. So some children are taller or smaller than other children. Which is the tallest child in this photo? (Answer on page 31.)

When you grow up you will probably be about the same height as your **parents**. If your parents are medium **height**, you probably will be too.

Bones

Bones are hard and strong. They give your body its shape. Without bones, you would flop like a jelly. Your bones grow longer and thicker as you grow.

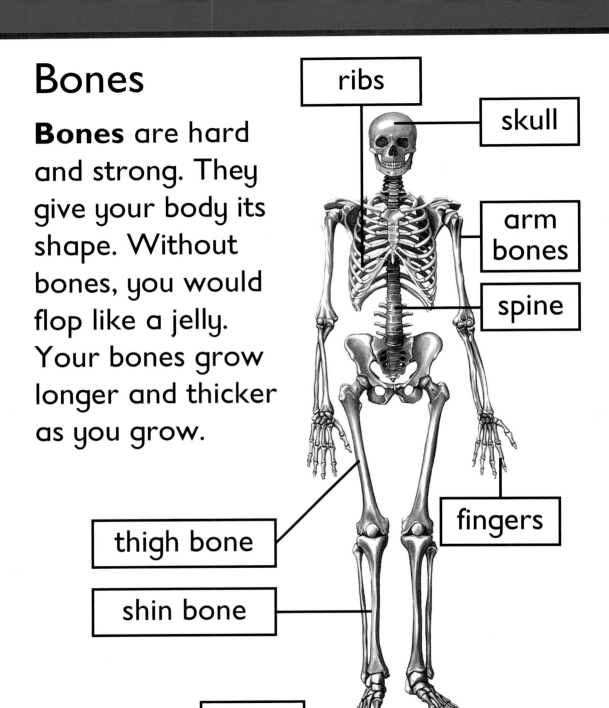

ribs

skull

arm bones

spine

fingers

thigh bone

shin bone

toes

The bones in your **spine** allow you to twist and to bend forwards and backwards. Whose spine is bending forwards the most? (Answer on page 31.)

Cells

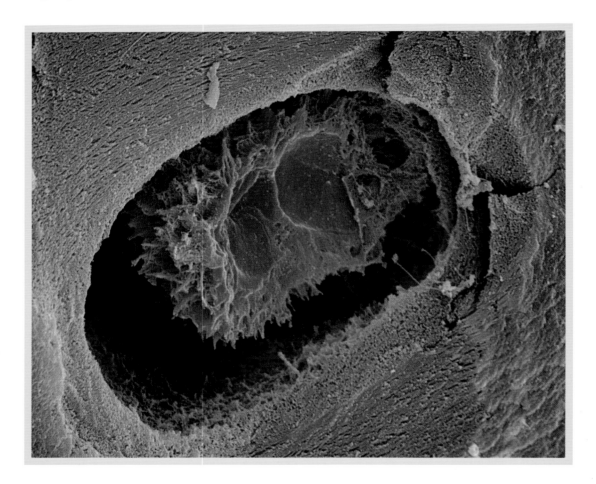

Your body is made up of millions of different kinds of **cells**. This is a bone cell. Cells are so small you need a **microscope** to see them.

Cells are like building blocks. Different parts of your body get bigger by adding on extra cells. Your body makes millions of new cells every day.

Two sets of teeth

When you were born, your first set of teeth was hidden in your **gums**. They slowly pushed through the gums. A second set formed behind them.

Your first set of teeth begin to fall
out when you are about six years
old. They are replaced by bigger
teeth from your second set.

Hair and nails

Hair grows faster than most other parts of your body. Some people allow their hair to grow long. Others have it cut every few months.

Nails grow quickly too. They grow from **cells** in the skin. This baby is having her nails cut to stop them from growing too long.

Healthy food

You need to drink water and eat several kinds of food. These will help you to stay healthy and grow well. Different foods help your body in different ways.

Eating spaghetti and cheese gives
you the **energy** you need to play.
Cheese also contains **protein**.
Proteins are special substances
that your body needs to grow.

Food that helps you to grow

Meat, fish and eggs contain a lot of **protein**. Cheese and beans contain lots of protein too. You should eat some protein food at every meal.

Bread, rice and lentils also contain some protein. If you do not get enough protein, you will not grow so tall. Which of the foods below contain protein? (Answer on page 31.)

Food that helps your bones

These foods all help your **bones** to grow long and strong. They contain a substance called **calcium**. Calcium in your bones makes them strong.

Calcium also makes your teeth stronger. But you still need to clean your teeth twice a day to keep them healthy.

Thinking and learning

As children grow older, they begin to think and to learn different things. This young child is learning to speak and to use his hands.

As you get older, you can do more difficult things. You also learn to read, write and to do sums. Your **mind** never stops growing!

Glossary

bones hard parts of the body, underneath the skin and flesh

calcium something in food that makes your bones and teeth hard and strong

cells very small building blocks that make up the different parts of the body

energy power to move and to do things

gums the flesh around your teeth

healthy being well and with all the parts of the body working properly

height how tall you are

microscope a tool that allows you to look at things that are normally too small to see

mind the part of the brain that knows and thinks

parents your mother and father

protein something that your body needs to build new cells. It is found in some foods.

spine back bone

toddler young child between about one and three years old

Answers

page 12
The girl on the left is the tallest child.

page 15
The spine of the girl on the right is bending forwards the most.

page 25
Both the eggs and the bread contain protein.

Index

Titles in the *My World of Science* series include:

Hardback   0 431 13700 5

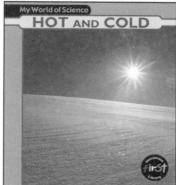

Hardback   0 431 13715 3

Hardback   0 431 13712 9

Hardback   0 431 13704 8

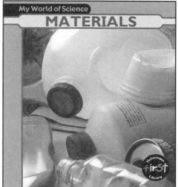

Hardback   0 431 13701 3

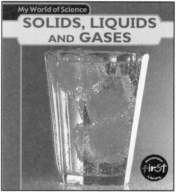

Hardback   0 431 13702 1

Hardback   0 431 13714 5

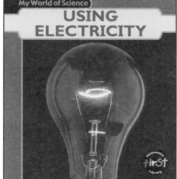

Hardback   0 431 13716 1

WATER

Hardback   0 431 13703 X

Find out about the other titles in this series on our website www.heinemann.co.uk/library